TASSANDRA BARNABY

Ethereal Whispers

"From The Enchantress Behind Whispers Of love"

First published by Tassandra Barnaby 2024

Copyright © 2024 by Tassandra Barnaby

All rights reserved. No part of this publication may be reproduced, stored or transmitted in any form or by any means, electronic, mechanical, photocopying, recording, scanning, or otherwise without written permission from the publisher. It is illegal to copy this book, post it to a website, or distribute it by any other means without permission.

First edition

ISBN: 9798330318001

This book was professionally typeset on Reedsy.
Find out more at reedsy.com

Contents

Revealing Souls: Writers' Journeys Through Adversity and Self-love

"Writers' works reveal their souls. Every facet of their everyday lives."

"Everyone...Every aspect of their mental makeup."

"To emerge stronger than ever after adversity, you must change course, heal, and then strive forward."

"Self-love is at the core of every happy life."

As We Blossom

"Life unfolds with the delicate grace of a flower in my garden, each petal a testament to the sentimental beauty we cherish."

"In the ocean's embrace, I blossomed like a flower."

"I shall not wither; I will bloom anew, rising like flowers from the depths of my soul."

Embrace the brilliance within your life. Celebrate its beauty and seize every opportunity with gratitude and joy. You cultivate inner light, emitting positivism that inspires others to glow. Let us cherish each moment, embracing the limitless potential for growth and happiness.

Introduction

The book Ethereal Whispers is a captivating compilation that blends poignant poetry with insightful quotes. It skillfully navigates profound emotions and musings, offering a deeply personal journey of self-discovery and introspection. The eloquence of verse and the wisdom of quotes guide readers to self-expression and inner peace, making it an exquisite fusion of poetry and heartfelt guidance. This collection takes readers on a heartfelt journey through the human soul, exploring the beauty of language and inviting them to find comfort in carefully crafted words.

"Ethereal Whispers weaves poetry and quotes into a journey of self-discovery and inner peace, guiding readers through the profound beauty of language."

Dedication

I am lucky because I have a supportive network of family and friends. They have always shown genuine care and support. Their encouragement and wisdom have been pivotal in my writing journey. They have boosted my confidence and fostered my growth.

I want to thank Kathleen Edouard, Albert Carter, and Celine Briggs for their unwavering support and insightful feedback. They have helped me with my writing. My husband, Danville Barnaby, and my sister, Petergay Ferguson, are my unwavering pillars of strength. Their constant encouragement fuels my passion.

I also want to express my gratitude to Latoya Brewster and Annelise McDowell. Their support during my college years was invaluable. It played a significant role in my development as a writer.

My family and friends have fueled my dreams with steadfast commitment. Their trust and faith in my abilities drive me.

"Your encouragement is the wind beneath my wings that propels me toward my goals."

Tribute to my younger self

My love for God fuels my awareness. It guides me as a thoughtful woman. Since my youth, I have immersed myself in literature and poetry. I did this to explore and understand the world. Tassandra, you can rest assured—we have reached our goal. I have fulfilled my lifelong dream of becoming a published poet.

"Your greatest supporter in life is yourself. Only you can."

"'Turn your dreams into reality and propel them into existence."

Biography

I was raised in Jamaica on December 13, 1985, amidst the island's stunning shores and rich cultural heritage. My life took a new direction when I moved to the United States at a young age to join my mother. Adjusting to a new culture and lifestyle was challenging, but it shaped my resilience and adaptability.

My professional journey began as a hospital cashier, where I learned the value of patience and empathy through interactions with patients and healthcare staff. Despite this rewarding experience, my passion for numbers led me to pursue an accounting degree at Quincy College. Graduating in 2017 with a two-year degree underscored my determination and commitment to my career.

A pivotal moment came when a writing course ignited my interest in poetry, revealing it as a profound medium for self-expression and reflection. This discovery complimented my passion for fashion, which I view as a canvas for creativity and personal expression.

In addition to these pursuits, I find joy in traveling, which allows me to forge connections and create lasting memories. Reading and literature continually expand my horizons, while music—mainly R&B, Reggae, and Soca—infuses my life with energy and joy.

"My experiences in hospital finance have shaped my time as a poet. Each day there taught me the value of empathy and resilience. These roles were not jobs. They were chapters. They enriched my poetry with humanity and understanding."

Whispers of resilience: Embracing Life's Journey Through poetry

Each breath blesses us in the tapestry of life. To embrace the unknown, take chances, and test. Fear not the journey, for living is our dance, In our hands alone, destiny's chance.

Each soul wrestles with shadows, and battles in the night, Yet through the darkness, we emerge, seeking light. Nature's beauty, is a balm for every scar, In its splendor, life's charm shines from afar.

Blood red stains our paths, and trials we face with grace, But in each struggle, we find our rightful place. Embrace this gift, this fleeting, precious time, For in life's moments, our most authentic selves shine.

"When I write poetry, it expresses my deepest emotions."

"A successful sentence hits like a punch or bursts with vivid imagery."

"Capture words, do not sip them, savor them."

The verses celebrate the deep beauty and strength in life's complex tapestry. It does this through vivid imagery and poignant metaphors. It explores the courage to face darkness and the comforting, healing power of nature. Each poem invites readers to embrace fleeting but precious moments. It urges them to savor the rich language. Language captures human emotions and experiences.

Embrace Your Qualities: Strength And Weakness in pursuit of dreams

"Embrace being your strength and weakness. Never let anyone undermine your dreams. They do so because they fail to see their worth or your growth potential."

*"The higher we soar in life, the more critics we attract.
Let their doubt fuel your determination."*

"Be the catalyst for change in your life. Don't let fear chain you down; let it fuel your transformation."

"Love without expectation. Your light will always lead you forward, regardless of an other's view."

Quote 1: It emphasizes embracing one's strengths and weaknesses. It highlights the importance of self-acceptance and resilience. These traits are key to achieving one's dreams, despite external doubt.

Quote 2: It encourages the use of criticism as motivation. This helps you soar higher in life. It displays determination and resilience in the face of adversity.

Quote 3: Stresses the importance of overcoming fear to start personal transformation. It positions fear not as a hindrance but as a catalyst for growth.

Quote 4: It promotes unconditional love and self-guided positivist. It suggests that growth should not depend on outside validation.

Navigating Life's Seasons

"Just as the world evolves with the seasons, so do our lives mirror this perpetual cycle. As the environment transforms, we adapt and grow, reflecting the vitality of the land. Our minds guide us, navigating the voyage of life where we seek and redefine our path."

Chapter One

Under the spell

Begins with thought-provoking quotes. The quotes set the stage for exploring alcohol's effects. The poems in this chapter explore how alcohol affects actions and decisions. They offer a thoughtful and detailed look at its impact on human behavior.

Intoxication: The lingering impact of liquor

"Intoxication: The Lingering Impact of Liquor"

"Let my love overflow like wine from a brimming cup."

"Romance is the poetry of heartbeats, written in whispers and felt in every touch."

Quote 1: "Intoxication: The Lingering Impact of Liquor" examines the deep effects of alcohol. It explores its lasting impact on the mind and body.

Quote 2: This quote evokes the idea of abundant love and passion. They overflow, like wine from a full cup. It suggests generosity and enough to express love and emotions. It draws a parallel between the effects of wine and the power of deep affection.

Quote 3: This phrase captures the heartfelt core of romantic connection. It likens romance to poetry, emphasizing relationships' subtle and tender aspects. The imagery of heartbeats, whispers, and touch shows the richness of romantic connections. It highlights the intoxicating effect of love and closeness.

Echoes of Intoxication: A Night Remembered

On a sultry July eve,
    when the humidity's warmth did cling,
    I sought refuge in Tolkien's world,
    where heroes sing.

Pages turned, tales unfolded,
    time lost its hold, as
    I savored each word;
    My heart and soul became whole.

A distant chime, a clarion call,
    my phone did ring,
    Kyle's voice, a gentle breeze,
    my solitude did sing.

"Hello,"
    I replied as plans took shape in the air,
    a night of freedom beckoned,
    with laughter and shared care.

I rose, refreshed,
    donned attire for the night,

A midnight silhouette,
with a smile and all its might.
Then, a thunderous knock,
a plea from a friend in need, Kyle,
with Grey Goose and spirits that would proceed.

"Let's go out,"
she exclaimed, eyes aglow with delight,
Adventure awaited, under the moonlight's Silver light.
Unplanned steps we took, hand in hand we strolled,
Two souls without a care, as the night's secrets unfold.

Timeless Glow

The light within our romance beams clear,
  A crystal gleams bright in his gaze,
  Tender skin meets skin,
  It is intimate and near.

He is my white wine, my brown-skinned delight,
  I drift on his love, lost in lust's embrace,
  My favorite drink, a light breeze at night,
  Caressing my mind with its gentle grace.

In our moments, perfectly timed,
  He scrolls through my timeline,
  devoted and kind,
  Whispering with a touch of the divine.
  I am his skyline, eternally bright.

Pure Radiance

In the glow of his eyes, serenity finds me
   His touch, a gentle breeze,
   grants a sweet release of our love, clear,
   shines bright and true
   Souls entwined, body to body, me, and you

He, my white wine, my delight in brown skin
   Intoxicated daily and nightly by his love's spin
   In his arms, secure and safe, I feel
   His love, a sweet melody, pure and real

With each moment, our love does grow
   Like a delicate flower in sunlight's soft glow
   Together, solid, and bright, we stand
   In our romance, light shines, hand in hand

I am his, and he is mine
   In this love, together, we shine
   A beacon in the night, so right
   Our love is forever pure and bright.

19

Echoes of regret: Poetry of choices and redemption

Your words paint a picture of the pain,
   Of choices made and the weight they sustain.
   The room spins, a dizzying haze,
   As you struggle to find your way.

Your heart beats heavy with regret,
   Each throb reminds us of what we have met.
   The liquor, a poor solace found,
   A fleeting escape from the truth unbound.

But in this moment, lost and alone,
   You must confront the choices you have made.
   The memories of what could have been,
   Haunting whispers in your ear, unseen.

Will you rise above this haze of night,
   Or will the weight of your choices hold you tight?
   Only time will tell, as the dawn breaks near,
   And the liquor's hold begins to clear.

Highway To Redemption: Poetry of life's fast lane

Speeding down the highway, bottle in hand,
  The rush of wind against my skin,
  Long journey behind, pain eased as death
  knocks at the car window.

The road unwinds into the distance.
  The road unwinds into the distance,
  disappearing.

A dark and twisting path to the beyond,
  Life flashed by in a blur.

The taste of Hennessy on my lips,
  A bittersweet reminder of the past,
  memories and regrets intertwine.

The hum of the engine beneath me,
  A lullaby of power and freedom,
  The burn of cognac soothes the soul.

I see the flash of red and blue lights,

As death creeps closer, eager, and relentless,
Speeding down the highway towards the unknown.

The shadows of my past loom large,
   haunting me with every passing mile,
   But I push harder on the gas pedal.

The world outside blurs into nothingness,
   A whirlwind of colors and shapes,
   As I hurtled towards my destination.
   The bottle slips from my grasp,
   Shattering against the floor,
   As death finally catches me in its cold embrace.

But as the darkness closes in,
   I find a strange sense of peace,
   Knowing that my journey is finally at an end.

Shadows and Spirits: Reflections in Neon Light

I sit in this bar, feeling down,
And I sip a cup of White Rum.
The liquid burns as it goes down.

The neon lights flicker above,
Casting shadows on my troubled soul.
I drown my sorrows in each sip,
Hoping the numbness will bring peace.

Savoring the essence of spirits

Allow me to speak more on this matter,
  During drowsy sex and scorching heat,
  I find myself filled with joy and laughter,
  Even the rain cannot bring me defeat.

Love is a force that knows no bounds,
  It colors the world in countless hues,
  At this moment, no location surrounds,
  If love is what I choose.

Tonight, I dance and lose myself,
  In the rhythm of the pounding beat,
  I let go of doubts and fears on the shelf,
  And embrace the passion that is so sweet.

My lips may speak without restraint,
  But my heart is open and true,
  I will not let anyone taint,
  The love that flows between us two.

So let my rump shake the night away,
  Let my words be bold and free,
  In the end,

it is love that will stay,
And that is all that matters to me.

25

Drunk In love and Honey tea

My Beloved, As we journey together,
   know that I am your steadfast companion.

Like a rose,
   I will bloom with each shift in our circumstances.
   My name whispered, is Hennessy.

Allow me to offer you a shot glass,
   a vessel for you to sample the essence of my spirit.

In exchange,
   I ask for a bottle of creamy liquor and a playful spin, sideways.
   Feel free to twist me as you desire; I am yours.

Darling,
   understand the depth of my admiration for you.

I remember the moment vividly spilling
   honeyed tea as you recited lyrics, your laughter echoing joyously.

The sight of us in a moving GIF,
   sharing a fluffy kiss midst distant clouds evoked a feeling akin to caressing
   my body, drunk in love with you.

Honeyed whispers and Whiskey kisses

Like honey, my dearest,
   You are a sweet man.
   Sweet as honey,
   I adore a dashing male.

With a splash of whiskey,
   The flavor of his sweet lips is my cocktail.
   Like the sun's warmth during the winter,
   Our love is a comforting and refreshing presence
   that brings out the best in us.

Everything I need to know is in his eyes.
   I enjoy peering inside because it confirms my identity as his honey.
   Our love is not a sweet cocktail; it is a complex blend of flavors.
   Your whiskey's edgy flavor brings out the smooth,
   velvety depth of my love when you savor it.

Yes, dear.
   Yes, dear.

He reaches out to me with one hand,
   Asking me to smother his lips in honey kisses.
   The other holds a bowl of sweet stuff from which he steals taste.

Velvet skin and gentle lies: A journey through drinking and redemption

My skin is so silky,
    And I have such a friendly disposition.
    My drinking began at lunchtime and has continued ever since.

I consume a constant flow of beverages from dawn till dusk.
    Even though it was raining,
    I went ahead and drank.

I have soft,
    Velvety skin and a gentle demeanor.
    And now that I am sober, the guilt is eating me alive,
    like it did when I drank all night long, not on red wine but also powder.

My skin is so silky,
    And I have such a friendly disposition.
    I have given up drinking hard liquor with those.
    Scorching fumes rise and they voice minute concerns instead.
    Trivial lies instead.

My skin is so silky,
    And I have such a friendly disposition.
    We cannot rest and allow our bodies to take their toll.

While consumed by the spirits of the wine we drink.

Time corrodes our bodies,
    The passage of time will inevitably wear us down,
    So why can't we chill out and let it happen?

I have soft,
    Velvety skin and a gentle demeanor.
    My laughter interrupts the calm chatter around me.
    Allow these dialogues to transport us to the unexpected regions of our
hearts.
    Let them be honest and enlightening
    like the sun coming up over our location
    or the greenest grass soaking up more chlorophyll.

My skin has a luxurious silkiness.
    I am a charming individual.
    We will become intoxicated by our poetry,
    And our dance partner will be the melody of our sorrows.
    Let us upload all these on the new edition of our website.

Storms Within: A Dance with Demons and Spirits

As far as I can tell,
     Only I can see the storm brewing outside,
     Dark clouds swirling ominously, pregnant with rain.

I fear the distant rumble of thunder,
     its echoes reverberating,
     As if each sound wave carries the weight of
     my internal strife.

My muscles tense coiled like springs.
     I resemble a crimson-
     eyed specter haunted by shadows that only I perceive.

Two bottles of Cognac VSOP and Molly to chase serotonin,
     A desperate attempt to quiet the storm within.

The night unfolded under a canopy of chilling air,
     Clouds brooding overhead, their darkness palpable,
     And my blood simmering with a restless energy,
     Yet my cheeks, tinged blue, crave the absent warmth of the sun.

In my mind,
    Flashes of light pierce through the fog,
    A chaotic dance where clarity struggles to emerge.

Against a friend's insistence,
    I downed the amber liquid,
    Its taste obliterated in an instant,
    replaced by a bitter aftertaste,
    Of vomit lingering on my tongue,
    a cruel reminder.

Like embalming fluid, it entombs me,
    Preserving me in a dreadful stillness,
    While a carousel of scents unfurls,
    From sweet vanilla to the deep oak of aged spirits.

It tastes of fig newtons soaked in rubbing alcohol,
    Forcing its way down my throat like a bitter cudgel,
    An intoxicating dance of flavors, a testament to its price.

Amidst the haze, a whisper of mortality lingers,
    Even in my decisive moments,
    I discern its age,
    In the nuances of each sip, each burn,
    Yet skepticism lingers, doubting its journey,
    From casks to convenience store shelves,
    In a bottle that may never have known the patience of time.

Secrets of the night

In the fading glow of daylight's embrace,
   My love returns, a gentle solace in flight.
   our gaze, a silent vow, a shared space,
   No thoughts of sleep, just the warmth of night.

A roll of leaves, a blend of tobacco's grace,
   A shared moment, a bond in the moon's soft light.
   No need for sleep as we wander, no place,
   In the quiet of our home, our hearts ignite.

Morning breaks, a tender dawn,
   Last night's revelry was a gentle ache.
   I rise early, the world reborn,
   Embracing flaws, the morning's wake.
   Together, in love's steady flight,
   Through highs and lows, a shared delight.

Amber Whispers: Poetry in the embrace of liquor

In the haze of amber dreams,
    Whiskey whispers weave their spell.
    Words stumble, slurred and sweet,
    Like drunken secrets, I cannot keep.

Each sip ignites a fire within,
    Melting walls of doubt and sin.
    In the amber depths, truths unfold,
    Tales of love and stories told.

The world rotates on its axis with every swallow.
    Inhibitions fade, and courage grows.
    Liquor-laced verses paint the night,
    A symphony of blurred delight.

Oh, liquor, muse of reckless charms,
    You coax the heart with open arms.
    In your embrace, we lose control,
    In your warmth, we find our soul.

But dawn will break this spellbound trance,
    Leaving echoes of the drunken dance.

Yet memories linger, bittersweet,
Of poetry under the influence of liquor's heat.

Shadows and stars: A journey through despair and hope

As I reach for the stars above
   The darkness below swallowed up my shadow.
   Branches crack beneath my weight
   Echoes of my past haunt me
   Life's burdens weigh heavy on my soul.

I seek solace in the warmth of whiskey.
   No mixer to dilute the pain within
   A fire raged inside, burning me alive.

The chill of the night surrounds me
   Yet my body burns with fever.
   Uncertainty clouds my future.
   But with each tear shed, a release.

I wash away my sorrows in a river of tears.
   Drowning in the depths of my despair
   Hoping to find peace in the shadows.
   As I gain into the star.

Chapter Two

Mystery

Opens with quotes that underscore its central theme of mystery. The chapter covers plans and schemes. Mystery shrouds each one. They show the uncertain and intriguing nature of the events.

Revelations In shadows

"Where truth ends, mystery begins, dangling on the precipice of revelation."
"Darkness hides truths that only light can reveal."

Quote 1: This quote reveals the gap between what we understand and the secrets that still must be unveiled. It suggests that mysteries emerge at the boundary of revealed truths. When we reach the limits of our knowledge, we encounter the unknown. It is a space full of discoveries and unanswered questions. This boundary is not a definitive end but rather a threshold teetering on the brink of new revelations. It makes us curious and eager to explore. It invites us beyond the familiar into mysterious realms beyond our understanding.

Quote 2: Here, darkness symbolizes ignorance or concealment. It contrasts with the illuminating power of light. Light represents knowledge, understanding, and clarity. In this metaphor, darkness veils reality, keeping certain truths hidden from view. We illuminate obscured areas to expose hidden truths and gain understanding. This quote underscores the trans-formative power of enlightenment and the pursuit of knowledge. It suggests that by exploring and asking, we can dispel ignorance's shadows and reveal the truths beneath. This fosters a deeper understanding of the world.

Navigating the Soul's Current

As I rise from the darkness,
   The wind whispers secrets from the sea,
   Brushing my skin as I dive beneath the surface,
   Lost at sea, adrift in thought.

My journey through time and space,
   Embracing life's unfolding mystery,
   Each wave a mirror of uncertainty,
   Yet I drift, letting the current guide me.

The stars above glitter in the night sky,
   A reminder of the boundless unknown,
   But at this moment, I am free,
   A sailor of the soul, exploring the depths within.

I am not adrift but anchored.
   To the beauty of the present moment,
   And as I rise with the tides,
   I find solace in the darkness,
   embracing life's mystery.

Whispers Of Escape

The whirl is like a prison's grip,
    A maze where troubled thoughts slip.
    The world, a bridge now fallen,
    A fragile path I'm drawn upon.

Trapped on this unforgiving land,
    No easy escape at hand.
    My mind drifts in disarray,
    Lost in a storm, swept away.

Debt looms like a shadowed threat,
    A burden is hard to forget.
    I wonder when it will strike,
    And my world will shift and spike.

Adrift in uncertainty's sea,
    There is no clear horizon, only debris.
    A prisoner in a world so grim,
    Where hope seems weak and dim.

Yet I will not be overthrown,
    I will not be left alone.
    I'll chart my course, come what may,
    And conquer doubt to find my way.

The Mystery Of Unrequited Love

It's a mystery to love someone
    who does not love you back?

The tears you shed behind closed doors fail to mend a heart left broken.

You give your all,
    yet receive nothing in return— a one-sided love.

It's a pain that cuts deep,
    leaving scars that never heal.

Still,
    you cling to a fragile hope that someday,
    they might see the love you offer and reciprocate in kind.

But until then, you carry on
    with a heavy heart and a soul that yearns
    for a love that may never be— a mystery of unrequited love.

Mysteries of love: Embracing joy and pain

Love is such a mystery.
  A puzzle we cannot solve.
  It is joy and its misery.
  A journey we revolve.

Love is pain that cuts deep.
  Leaving scars upon our soul
  Yet, in our hearts, it keeps.
  A flame that makes us whole

Love is tears we shed.
  For moments lost and gone
  We follow them instead.
  To a brighter dawn

Love is unknown and uncertain.
  A path we walk blind.

But in its embrace,
  we are certain.
  True love we will find.

So, let us embrace the mystery.
  Of love's twists and turns

For in its complexity A lesson,
we will learn.

42

Midnight Conundrum

It has been a long day,
   A cosmic dance with Star man,
   Yet my soul remains uneasy.

Chilled body, restless mind,
   Tonight, mysteries unravel.
   Within the shadows of my being.

Echoes Of Memories

I yearn for her warm, comforting touch,
    For the gentle lullabies that once did soothe,
    For the way, she would whisper words of love and peace,
    And fill my heart with joy and release.

But now, the world is dark and gray,
    And I am adrift, lost, without a way,
    To navigate the grief that consumes me whole,
    To find my bearings, to regain my soul.

I beg for a sign, a whispered word,
    A glimpse of her beauty, a love unheard,
    But all I find is emptiness and pain,
    A sorrow that gnaws like a persistent stain.

Yet still, I will visit her graveside each night,
    And lay my heart upon her silent light,
    For in her memory, I find a spark,
    A glimmer of hope that guides me back to who I am.

One day, she will return to me,
    In dreams or whispers, wild and free,
    Until then, I will hold on to what remains,
    We sustained the love we shared and the memories.

Finding home in the night's embrace

In twilight's hush, where shadows play.
  I wander, lost, with my heart astray.
  The crickets' lullaby, a mournful sway
  Echoes through the darkness of my day
  The road ahead, a winding stream
  That flows to nowhere,
  yet I must dream.

Of a light that guides me through the night
  And leads me to the warmth of morning's light.

In the darkness, I find my strength.
  A resilience that lengthens with each step
  For in the unknown, I find my voice.

A whispered prayer that breaks the noise
  Of fear and doubt that seeks to claim
  My soul's true path, my heart's actual name

And when the crickets' song grows still
  And all is dark, and all is chilly.
  I will find my way, and I will find my home.
  Where love and light will make me whole once more.

Breaking Free: A journey from darkness to light

In despair,
    I feel trapped in a nightmare,
    Facing abuse and pain from a man's rage and might.

With each passing day, blows rain down,
    Hiding tears, carrying a heavy heart, wearing a frown.
    Who will rescue me from this brutality's plight?
    From this prison, who will set me free from this endless fight?

Then, a realization sparks within.
    The key to healing lies beneath my skin.
    To break free from torment's grasp,
    I must find courage within and clasp.

With strength and resolve,
    I stand tall,
    Breaking away from his grip, from his toxic thrall.

Taking back control, slipping from the dark eclipse.
    I walk away, head held high, with a final kiss.

Closing the door on pain and sorrows might,
Welcoming a future bathed in light.
No longer a victim, no longer in fear's sight,
I break free, reclaiming my spirit, pure and bright.

In newfound peace's quiet embrace,
I rise like the sun, with gentle grace.
From shadows that once clouded my days,
To a life where my soul dances and sways.

With each step forward,
I grow stronger,

The past no longer binds me.
I am bolder. No longer defined by the scars I bore.

I am complete;
I soar. In my journey's tapestry, resilience sewn,
Replacing dread with strength shown.

Every word, every verse sings of my fight,
Of reclaiming my voice, of finding my light.
Let the world witness my story unfold,
Of courage, hope, and being bold.

In the echoes of my healing plea,
I am reborn, pure, and accessible.

Rising Above: A journey of courage and liberation

I soar above the clouds, my spirit unbound.
  No longer tethered to the ground.
  I am a warrior, fierce and strong.

Shunning the darkness, singing a new song
  I am the hero of my tale.
  No longer weak, no longer frail,
  I am the one who saves the day.
  By having the courage to walk away

From the abusive man who sought to destroy
  My spirit, my soul, my joy I am a phoenix reborn, I rise from the ashes.

With a fierce determination,
  no longer torn.
  My spirit soars, my heart sings
  As I embrace the freedom that freedom brings
  I am a survivor, a warrior, a bold Breaking free from the darkness, no
longer cold

I am a victor, not a victim.
  Shining bright, my light never dims.

I am free, I am strong.
I am me, where I belong.

With courage and strength,
   I walked away.
   Held back, no longer prey.
   To the darkness that once enveloped me I am free.
   I am finally free.

Whispers in the dark: Finding home midst the forest

Lost in the dark forest.
  Whispers surround,
  Twisting paths, shadows profound.

Echoes of time lost and unknown,
  Guiding light, where has it flown?

Steps slow, leaves whisper,
  Moonlight flickers and stars pass by.
  A labyrinth of silence, a maze of fear,
  The heartbeat quickens, and the breath is unclear.

Yet through the gloom, a glimmer appears,
  A distant beacon, dispelling my fears.
  Each step forward, each breath I take,
  The forest speaks, its secrets awake.

Finally, a clearing, a path revealed,
  Home awaits, with warmth concealed.
  Through trials endured in the forest deep,
  I find my way, my soul to keep.

Ethereal shadow: Unveiling the secrets of a forsaken town

In whispers, I return to this forsaken town,
   A place where memories of childhood linger
   yet faded away like smoke.

I beckon Sally, my friend from days of yore,
   To join me in this desolate landscape,
   where time stands still.

As we wander, the air grows thick with shadows,
   And human forms dissolve,
   like mist at dawn's first light.
   A sudden flash of light,
   a brittle snap of wood,
   Illuminates the darkness as if a star had fallen.

The ground beneath us is a chasm of blackness deep,
   A void that swallows all, leaving only silence to keep.

Yet,
   in this abyss, a figure appears,
   ethereal and bright,

A woman with legs that shine like diamonds in the night.

Her face is a masterpiece of beauty,
   crafted with precision fine,
   Her eyes sparkle with mischief,
   like emeralds that glint in the mine.

If no one greets me back,
   I shrug and move on,
   My hand extended,
   only to find nothing but cold stone.

But then I touch her hand and discover it is not her skin,
   But something cold and artificial, like a doll's stiffened smile.

My steps are steady now, my confidence restored,
   For I have seen the truth behind the mask she wore.

She is lovable when she sheds her diva's disguise,
   And her charm shines through like sunlight breaking through dark skies.

But everything within her is as unsettling as a puppet's stare,
   Frozen in time, its eyes empty and cold as the dark air.

Shadows of love: A tale of moonlit terror

In the dim shadows where moonlight fades,
Unfolds a dark tale of sinister parades,
Whispers stir, sparking fears so deep,
In the heart of the night, secrets to keep.

Jonathan, a man with love enshrined,
His heart captured, his thoughts confined,
To Kim, fair and kind, a true beauty,
Yet shadows lurk, bound by the villain's duty.

A menacing figure with eyes ablaze,
Lurks in shadows, lost in the maze,
His silent steps, his presence cold,
A tale of terror yet to unfold.

Kim walks the streets, love in her heart,
Footsteps soft, a shiver at the start,
A chill runs deep, a whisper nears,
The villain's breath sparks fear.

Through dreary alleys, they flee,
From dread and darkness, trying to break free,
Time slips by, shadows combine,

In the villain's grip, hopes decline.

At each twist, the chase goes on,
  The villain's laughter, like a dark dawn,
  Fear and flight, in the night,
  Kim and love, escaping the fright.

But in the mist, at the end,
  A showdown, a twist to comprehend,
  Kim faces the villain's gaze,
  Protecting her love in a fearful daze.

As dawn breaks, the villain fades away,
  His icy grip, his chilling display,
  A mystery solved, hearts entwined,
  In Kim's embrace, love's refuge is defined.

Whispers in the night: A haunting encounter

He slips in, fingers crossed.
   Hoping no one sees him in the night's gloom.
   The wind howls loud,
   drowning out the rain's drum.

White drapes billow,
   revealing his frame in silhouette.

My heart stutters, my breath falters too
   His hand touches mine.
   My anxiety breaks through.
   Did he tarnish my reputation?
   My heart pounds with shame
   His breath is stale, making me dizzy,
   lost in this game.

His voice remains a whisper that haunts my ear.
   A fleeting presence that vanishes without a care
   Haiku of fear, haiku of dread In the darkness,
   where he fled.

Gratitude unveiled: A poetic reflection on life's gifts

A whispered thanks in the still of night,
    For the stars that twinkle with all their might,
    For the moon's gentle glow, a beacon bright,
    Guiding me through life's darkest plight.

For every breath, I take, for every beat,
    For every moment I am alive to meet,
    The world's vast wonder, the beauty it holds,
    A rich tapestry, woven with threads of gold.

For every tear I have cried,
    for every scar, For every lesson learned,
    for every star, That led me to this moment, to this place,
    I give thanks and acknowledge life's embrace.

Love shared, love true,
    For laughter and tears, for moments anew,
    For life's difficulties, for trials and strife,
    I give thanks for this precious gift of life.

Whispers of moonlight love: Sailing dreams in sultry nights

On sultry nights like these,
   when thunder whispers secrets to the sky
   My mind sails forth, a ship of dreams,
   to distant shores,

I would instead try.
   To reach the shores of desire,
   Where does love's lighthouse shine so brightly?
   And the gentle breeze carries scents of lavender, a siren's alluring light.

In this dream world,
   My heart beats fast as I chart a course, so fine.

With every stroke,
   my soul takes flight toward the one who is mine
   For in his eyes, a diamond glimmer, a treasure rare and true.
   A reflection of the beauty within, shining bright, for me and you.

The silver floral earrings sway like delicate vines on a tree
   As I wear my heart on my sleeve and let my soul be set free
   The spaghetti straps caress my skin like tender fingers on a flute.

Playing the melody of our love, a harmony so sweet and anew.

In this moonlit whispering night,
    where stars twinkle like diamonds, bright.
    I will anchor my ship of dreams and let our love take flight.

For in his arms is where I will find solace,
    where love's warmth will be my guide.
    And together, we will ride the waves of passion side by side.

Twilight's resolve: A journey through shadows

In twilight's hush, where shadows play,
 I search for solace, night's dark sway,
 The clock's relentless beat, a morbid rhyme,
 Echoes through my soul, a mournful chime.

The rustling leaves, a funeral sigh,
 As I wander lost, with tears to dry,
 The stranger emerged, a shadowy figure,
 A harbinger of fate, a bitter storm.

Years have passed, yet death still waits,
 At my bedside, an unwelcome guest, irate,
 I curse the silence, the delay,
 As my soul begins its final sway.

In this desolate land, where darkness reigns,
 I feel lost and weary, with fading traces.
 But even in the void, a spark remains,
 A flicker of life, a desperate refrain.

The night is cold, the stars are dim,
 But still, I search for hope within,

A glimmer of light, a gentle touch,
To guide me through this shadowed clutch.

As twilight fades and morning breaks,
I rise to face the dawn's embrace,
With courage newfound,
I stand, unbowed,
And face the future, unafraid and proud.

In twilight's hush, where shadows play,
I find my strength to light my way,
Through the darkest night,

I will find my sight,
In the end,
I will conquer the night.

The beast within a tale of shadows and sorrow

Beware the beast within my soul,
    Entrapped with no name or appearance,
    A creature alive and untamed,
    Still yearning for release from its chains.

The heaviness in the air,
    a burden to bear,
    Eclipsing the light and making it hard to breathe.
    All I have ever known is this wild creature inside,
    Its fierceness and primal nature are undeniable.

The repressed thoughts,
    a locked room within,
    Only unlocked by the key to rage and sin.
    Memories of pain and sorrow,
    Echoing in the shadows of tomorrow.

A face slashed open, a mother's death,
    The stench of evil tainting every breath.
    Since death is the only escape from this dark cell,
    I will watch the birds soar and bid farewell.

Winter's whispering secrets

The whispers of winter's chill begin,
  As Pauline folds her wings within,
  A symbol of the heart's retreat,
  When frosty winds and darkness meet.

The jet's white wings, a canvas bright,
  Against the blue, a canvas in sight,
  A reminder of life's grand design,
  A masterpiece that embodies sublime beauty.

The carriage rides, a misty veil,
  A sad scene, a tale to hail,
  A lone figure, lost in thought,
  Rain and wind conspire to bring about the change.

Anticipation builds, like embers high,
  As figures emerge through misty eyes,
  A coachman, a child, a mystery to share,
  Their journey begins with secrets to spare.

The young man's handshake, a glimpse to see,
  Through deep brown gloves, a mystery to me,
  The chilly air bites like a winter's sting,
  As Roy's small hand reaches out for warmth to cling.

And in the falling snow's sweet sigh,
Our steps become visible as the world goes by,
A fleeting moment, in the rain's gray haze,
A memory etched in the heart's daze.

Shadows of silence: Unveiling night's secrets

In no way can I divulge my genuine identity,
    Hidden in the shadows, unknown even to me.
    In the night, what exactly goes on within me?
    Dreams and fears swirl in the vast sea.

There are no limits to the thoughts that race,
    As I lay in my bed, in a quiet, peaceful space.
    My brown flesh feeling lost, abandoned, and alone,
    My true self remains hidden in the darkness.

The fan's hum and the snoring fill the air,
    As I lay there, wondering, lost in despair.
    Unable to escape the chaos in my mind
    Hoping someday, true peace I will find.

But for now, I keep my secrets hidden deep,
    In the dark of night, where my soul does weep.
    In no way can I reveal my identity,
    In the silence of the night, where my heart is free.

Echoes of love: A memory in silence

In the silence, I hear his cries,
   Echoes of love, now but a sigh.
   My words, once warm, like soup that stirs,
   Now lost in darkness, cold as ice.

A distant drumbeat,
   the sound of the ocean's roar,
   Carries me away, and my warmth gradually fades more.
   Holes in my form, like wounds that will not mend,
   Leaking life, like tears that never end.

In his heart, a grief so profound,
   A longing for the love we once found.
   He searches for solace in my touch,
   But he finds only emptiness, a hollow clutch.

I am a memory, a fleeting thought,
   A whispered name, an echo caught.
   My smile, like sunshine lost at sea,
   A distant dream, a memory to be.

Yet still, I hold on to what he has left of me,
   A shard of love, a memory to set free.
   For in his heart, my soul still resides,

A warmth that glows, a love that will not subside.

A warmth that glows, a love that will not subside.

River's harmony

A midst the furnace heat of twilight's glow,
   A siren's song echoed, soft and low.
   A young Susie's voice, like honeyed wine,
   Sweetened the air, and my heart entwined.

Her notes danced on the river's gentle stream,
   As I closed my eyes, my soul began to beam.
   My heart dissolved, consumed by a gentle, warm intensity.
   In harmony with her voice, my spirit started to grow.

The roar of water merged with her gentle tone,
   A symphony of joy, forever known.
   In that moment, time stood still, frozen in time,
   As our hearts beat as one, in perfect rhyme.

That chance encounter, a life-altering charm,
   A memory etched forever, a love-filled balm.
   For in Susie's song, I found my peace,
   A harmony that resonates, a soul that releases.

Echoes of eternity's highway: Tales from the road unwound

In the echoes of eternity's highway,
  We wander, lost in time and space,
  Seeking solace in the cracks and crevices,
  Where memories hide like fossils of the past.

The Road Unwinds, a twisting tale,
  Twisting and turning evermore,
  A labyrinth of asphalt and stone,
  Where tires screech and people wear their hearts.

Where tires screech and people wear their hearts.
  Of laughter, tears, and moments old,
  Of choices made, of paths untold,
  We have not yet discussed the roads not taken.

Yet, in this endless, winding way,
  We find ourselves, no matter what happens,
  For in each step, we find our feet,
  And in each mile, our hearts do meet.

As the journey stretches out before,

A vast canvas, a story to explore,
We will fill its cracks and crevices, too,
With tales of love, of dreams anew.

So let us drive, through rain and shine,
Through tunnels dark, through mountains divine,
And find the beauty in every bend,
For in this journey, our souls will mend.

Whispers of the night's realm

Within my heart, a dreamer dwells,
   Were imagination reigns supreme,
   At night, I wonder,
   lost in fantasies that unfold like a dream.

But dawn breaks and a radiant face appears,
   warm and bright,
   Filling my soul with joy and
   anticipation for the day's delight.

In slumber,
   I roam,
   a sleepwalking fantasist,
   seeking an isle to claim,
   Where morning's mystery will not disturb
   my peaceful night's name.

The thought of awakening,
   lost and alone,
   with no idea where to roam,
   Fills me with unease,
   a constant companion to
   my nocturnal home.

I will lie on sandy shores, breathing in the salty air,
Twirling strands of hair as the ocean
The breeze whispers secrets there.
I will bask in the sun's warm touch,
letting worries fade away,
But even in repose,
the fear of darkness lingers,
no matter what happens.

Chapter Three

Love

It begins with a quote on the nature of love and explores this theme through its poetry. The chapter is about aspects of love. It offers a rich tapestry of reflections and expressions.

Embracing Love: Quotes and Reflections

"Within the embrace of love, one feels its beauty. the one you cherish."

"Love is the sweetest gift and the most generous offering. It enriches the soul and brightens the heart."

Quote 1: This quote captures the deep essence of love. It highlights love's intense emotional resonance. When you share love with a cherished partner, you feel it.

Quote 2: This statement highlights love as a force that brings joy. It transforms and fulfills. Love enhances one's inner being and lights up life with its warmth and generosity.

Eternal Whispers in the Night

Night's stillness holds your tender touch,
  A memory that stays,
  A whisper in my ear,
  love so pure and sweet,
  Your kiss, a flame refusing to fade,
  Our hearts are entwined,
  forever connected in love.

With every caress, my senses awaken,
  Your words are a soothing melody to my soul,
  In your embrace, free to flourish,
  Our love orchestrates a harmony that makes
  I feel complete.

Caress my lips with yours,
  Let our love intertwine,
  With every breath, our passions merge.

Could it be you, the one my heart longs for?
  Are you the one with whom my soul shares secrets
  Under the night's quiet veil?

Is it you who ignites my desires like wildfire

In summer's heat?
Are you the one who quickens my pulse
Like a drumbeat in a lover's embrace?

Do you hear the whispers of my heart
Beating only for you?
Can you feel the warmth of my soul yearning
To be with you again?
If so, I am lost, forever entranced by your gaze.
And with each breath,

I will cherish this love born from endless days.
Am I the one your heart craves?
My heart finds its sweetest flame.
Oh, I hope I am, for in your eyes.

Blossom Of Love

Like a flower in bloom,
    With cherry sweetness on my lips,
    Your kisses, like cherry pie, grace my delicate skin.

Soft and tender,
    Each touch is a symphony of sensation,
    Igniting fireworks of passion within.

You are the breath of spring,
    Reviving my soul with every caress,
    Leaving me intoxicated by your love.

In your arms,
    I bloom,
    A delicate flower in the garden of your heart,
    Nourished by the sweetness of your affection.

Forever entwined,
    Like vines reaching for the sun,
    Our love blossoms endlessly,
    A fragrant reminder Of the sweetness we share.

Eternal Flame

The flame that burns so deep
In my heart, a constant heat,
A fire that sparks and never fades,
Brightening my soul with love's crusades.

Through trials and endless nights,
You are my beacon, my guiding light,
A spark that ignites with a flame so pure,
In the darkness, your love is my only cure.

Moments with you are the most incredible part,
You dwell forever in my heart,
Blood flows strong, a rhythmic song,
In your love, I know I belong.

You are the fire that warms my core,
A love that I cannot ignore,
In your embrace,
I find my ease,
It's the flame that will never cease

Sanctuary In Your Love

In a chaotic world, we find solace,
On this serene vacation, our hearts entwine,
Your arms, a refuge so peaceful,
Love's excellent breezes race through our minds.

I feel my dreams blossom within your embrace,
Warm and funky, filled with love's grace,
Your smile, a beacon that lights up my face,
As we share a meal, savoring wine's embrace.

In your soul's paradise, the sun shines bright,
Your lips, kissed by daylight's delight,
You are my shelter in life's storm,
In your love, I feel reborn.

No sky needs to fall at my feet,
In your embrace, peace tastes so sweet,
Midst the world's chaos, my sanctuary is you,
In your love, everything feels true.

Wings of Solace

In my arms, I find solace,
    A release that sets me free,
    Like wings soaring high,
    In the boundless sky's spree.

My spirit glows like rose quartz,
    Radiating love and light,
    Embracing the world with grace,
    A soul is pure and bright.

With a heart carved in charm,
    I wear it close to me,
    A token of love and warmth,
    Rich and deep for all to see.

In your eyes, the universe unfolds,
    Reflecting on my essence whole,
    We dance to our heartbeats' song,
    Lost in a love untold.

I am a free spirit, unafraid to fly,
    With you, I soar and explore,
    In the hue of a yellow canary,
    Peace resides forever.

Journey Of Love

Our love, a roller-coaster ride,
With twists and turns so wide,
Up and down, emotions churn,
A journey where hearts collide.

Passion ignites flames so bright,
In jealous eyes, never a blight,
Together, we float through life's maze,
Love's whispers forever in flight.

Surrounded by a happy glow,
Basking in each other's flow,
Kisses sweet as honey's grace,
Love's embrace, no harm to sow.

This love, a wild, beautiful stride,
Through highs and lows, side by side,
A journey we bravely ride,
With you, my love, as my guide.

Harmony Of Hearts

Your heart charges, mine,
   Symphonies of intertwined love,
   My heart's joyous journey swiftly alters.

Your heart, a bright rose gold,
   A beacon of warmth untold,
   Reflects your heartwarming fondness.

The glitter in my eyes,
   A reflection of our enduring love,
   Shines like a hundred sparkling diamonds.

Under moonlight's gentle glow,
   Our love continues to bloom,
   Infuse sweetness into the cadence of your voice.

I love you, In every shade and hue,
   In every way, my heart is yours, true.

Eternal Blossoms

Our love blooms through seasons,
Like the Blue Lace flower standing tall.
In the night's embrace, your face in dreams,
You are the flame that warms my heart in winter's thrall.

Finishing my thoughts with just a glance,
You know me deeply; our harmony is a song.
Smiling at the hearts around us that dance,
I love you more than any dish all day long.

Happy anniversary, my love,
Together, through storms and calm, we strive,
Our love, a garden ever in bloom,
I am grateful forever for your gift in my life.

Wings Of Love

Oh, sweetness,
 Sweet love's taste,
 Let us soar on Caribbean breezes,
 Our love, a blue morph butterfly,
 Spreading wings over oceans.

Our love will not fade to gray,
 Vibrant with colors,
 Curving us together,
 Our eyes are steadfast.

We show affection dynamically,
 Colorful as a rainbow,
 Drawing every gaze,
 Love is rare and authentic.

Dancing to our voices' melody,
 Joyous love, forever entwined,
 In a symphony of emotions,
 Our hearts beat as one.

Eternal Harmony

In the harmony of my life,
 I flourish beside you,
 Like the sun rising in our love's embrace.

Your love, a gentle melody,
 Caresses my soul,
 And my smile illuminates the night.

I am the diamond against your skin,
 Your cherished lady,
 The key that unlocks your heart's delight.
 In the warmth of spring,
 Your gaze sweetens like candy,
 And your kiss ignites my lips,
 A craving for pure delight.

Within your arms, I find refuge,
 Grace envelops me,
 In your eyes, my reflection shines.

In your love, I discover perfection,
 Together, hand in hand,
 We navigate life's joys and trials,
 For you are my reason, my love, my life.

Sunlit petals: A love story among daisies

In fields of sunlit gold, where daisies bloom,
  Your love unfurls a gentle, sweet perfume.
  Each petal whispers secrets soft and genuine,
  At every glance, I find myself anew.

Like daisies dancing in the morning light,
  Your laughter sparkles, chasing out the night.
  Soft heat radiates from every gentle caress,
  soothing cradles.

In your embrace,
  my heart forever stays.

Through storms that rage or calm of summer breeze,
  Your love, a steadfast bloom among the trees.
  In every moment, you are my guiding light,
  A love as sweet and pure as daisies bright.

So let us dance upon this meadow fair,
  Where daisies bloom, and love fills the air.
  Forever bound by nature's sweet embrace,
  Our love, a daisy field, a timeless grace.

Whispers of love: A journey through twilight

As petals unfold,
  our love takes flight.
  In this warm breeze,
  our hearts beat in sight.
  With every whisper,
  our love's gentle might
  Echoes through time,
  a love so bright

In this sweet surrender,
  We found our nest.
  Where love's whispers calm the restless breast
  And as the sun dips low,
  our love's desire
  Fades into the twilight, a burning fire.

Whispers of the night: Serenades and dreams

The night whispers secrets in my ear,
   Of distant lands and memories so dear,
   The stars above, a sparkling sea,
   Reflecting the expectations for our dreams.

The world lies still in quiet calm.
   As I stand here, my heart does keep,
   A rhythm beating, a melody sweet,
   A love song to the one who is hard to meet.

In the silence,
   I hear your name,
   A whispered promise, a love so tame,
   The moon above, a silver glow,
   Guiding me to the path we will go.

At this moment, time stands still,
   As I serenade the one, I love so ill,
   With every note, a piece of me goes,
   To the heart that beats with love that knows.

And when the night has gone by dawn,

And the world awakens from its dream born,
I will hold on tight to this serenade sweet,
And cherish the love that our hearts have met.

Beyond the horizon: Clara and jack's journey of love

Across the miles, their love did roam,
   A flame that burned, a heart that called home.
   Though distance separated, souls so strong,
   Their love remained where hearts did belong.

In whispers, they would share their deepest fears,
   And in each other's eyes, they would dry their tears.
   In the silence between calls, a heavy heart did bear,
   But love's persistence is a beacon to repair.

On moonlit nights, they would dance beneath the sky,
   Their love's rhythm beat as the stars went by.
   And when the dawn broke, with morning's golden light,
   They would whisper sweet nothings through the still at night.

Clara and Jack's love, a beacon of might,
   A shining star that guided through life's plight.
   For in each other's hearts, they found a home,
   A love that conquered distance, a love that made them whole.

Melodies of love: A symphony in the silence

In the silence of the night,
   I hear your sweet refrain.
   A melody that whispers sweet nothings, a gentle, loving rain
   Your smile, a ray of sunshine, warms my heart and soul.
   As our lips meet, fireworks of passion ignite,
   making me whole.

Like a river flowing through my veins, our love does grow.
   A harmony of heartbeats, a rhythm only we know.
   In your eyes, I see a beauty that is untouchable and bright.
   A love that shines like a beacon, guiding me through the night.

In your arms,
   I find my home, where love resides.
   Where every kiss is a celebration,
   Every touch is a symphony inside.

Your heart beats like a drum, keeping time with mine
   Our love unites in perfect harmony,
   resonating with celestial beauty.

Our love story is one for the ages, etched in my mind.

A memory that will forever linger,
like the scent of a sweet vine.

For in your eyes,
I see forever a love that is strong and true.
A bond that will forever be between me and you.

Symphony of love: A masterpiece in red

In my art, my heart, a masterpiece of love,
  With warmth and form, emotions rise and move,
  A portrait painted in shades of red,
  My soul leads high art with love.

My soul blooms, a symbol of love's sweet embrace,
  A melody through eyes, a warm and tender grace,
  Romantic love, universal and true,
  Soft within my chest, my love for you.

Let the rhythm of love's sweet refrain,
  Echo through the verses, like a gentle rain,
  In my art, my heart, love's beauty does impart,
  A symphony of love, a masterpiece, fine art.

Guided by your love

In the darkest night, when stars do fall,
  I will love you more than anything, my all.
  My beacon of light in the blackened sky,
  Guiding me through, never questioning why.

Your love is the wings that route me true,
  Carrying me on in all that I do.
  Your love shines bright in the depths of darkness,
  I will love you more than anything, day, or night.

Shadows of love: A journey through darkness

In the shadows, kiss me, my love,
　　Embraced by the darkness, let us move,
　　Wrapped in passion's tender hold,
　　Our hearts entwined, beating bald.

Though miles apart, love's path we trace,
　　Through battles fought, night and day embrace,
　　I am your soldier, fighting strong,
　　You, my princess, my guiding song.

In the shadows, kiss me, my love,
　　In the whispered night, our beacon thereof,
　　Let our love light the way,
　　Through darkness, to a brighter day.

Passion guides our longing flight,
　　Back to each other, in love's sweet light.
　　In shadows, above, we will rise,
　　United in love's tender ties.

Chapters of the heart: Embracing life's pen

In the chapters of our lives, we find.
    People who touch our hearts and minds
    They cherish their presence like an old book.
    Their absence felt, love undiminished.

But life moves on as pages turn.
    Sometimes, leaving our hearts to burn
    Watching them with someone new
    Feels like a dagger, painful and true.

Loving someone who does not love your back.
    It is like holding onto a cactus, a painful lack.
    Of reciprocity, of all we desire.
    Yet we must let go, our hearts on fire.

We are the authors of our tale.
    No one else can prevail.
    Take hold of life's pen, and author your own story.
    Embrace the pain, the love, the glory.

Love's pure fire

In the dreams of the night,
  you are my guiding light,
  A love so deep, a wondrous sight.

Your touch ignites a fire within my soul,
  A love so pure, making me whole.

This love transcends the measure of gold,
  It is in the warmth of every fold.

Through eternity's embrace, in every season,
  I cherish you without any reason.

As tomorrow may come and I close my eyes to sleep,
  You are the only one in deep dreams so deep.

Ephemeral Symphony

I curve my lips upwards, revealing no hints.
In the darkness where hope now lies,
My soul refuses to falter after you,
For new love is blind, yet so true.

No road signs to guide my way,
Navigating through love's dismay,
I have outgrown the pain, the broken heart,
Now, my tears are a canvas of art.

Yes, love may be blind, but I see,
The beauty in its mystery,
No styles or rules, pure emotion,
A symphony of love in constant motion.

Solace in your arms

I await your embrace, where peace is unsound.
   Love and fondness surge, visions of you appear,
   It is present, not in dreams, but within close reach.

Strolling past blooms in their vibrant array,
   Yearning for love's hues to brighten my day.
   My heart bursts with passion for you, my dear,
   Discovering a hidden beach, pristine and clear.

By the ocean's edge,
   I yearn to declare,
   Letting waves carry my love beyond comparison.
   In your arms, solace found, pure and true,
   Love is eternal, forever with you.

Melody of love

In love's embrace, our hearts find their place,
  Intertwined, eliminating the necessity for a
  distinct area. Like a river's song, our love flows free,
  An enthusiastic melody for all to see.

The sun shines bright when we are side by side,
  Kisses like sweet notes in love's perfect tide.
  Our love, rich and pure like a flavor divine,
  Endures in our cherished home, an eternal shrine.

With each breath, roses' scent fills the air,
  Passion ignites, composing a love affair.
  In the heat of sensation, our hearts entwine,
  In perfect joy, our love's embrace is divine.

Thus, in love, we flourish, our spirits aglow,
  In hues and harmonies, our love does grow.
  A symphony sweet, pure, and ever sure,
  Forever and always, our love will endure.

Whispers of love

When the wind blows, my love,
    seek refuge in your embrace,
    Where gentle breezes whisper love's tender grace.

I will hold you near, a haven from the storm's rage,
    My heart finds solace in your arms, a sanctuary on life's stage.

I will kiss you like the stars that sparkle in the night,
    In our love's celestial dance, our spirits take flight.
    Entwined in harmony, a symphony of grace,
    Bound by eternal vows in this sacred space.

Forever I will love you, beyond time's gentle sway,
    Through trials and triumphs, beside you, I will stay.
    In your arms, my soul is calm and finds tranquility.
    Your love has left an everlasting blessing in my heart.

Bound by love

Love, patient, and kind, a binding force divine,
  Yet within it lies a pain, deep and intertwined.
  Grief pours out in torrents, anguish deepens.

But love's embrace in solace we seek.
  Loving you, a voyage through stars untold,
  Each kiss makes a sensation, sweet and bold.
  Emotions weave a tapestry, connection deep,
  Binding our hearts in love's eternal keep.

My love for you is boundless,
  knows no end, In your arms, tranquility, a cherished blend.
  Through life's ebbs and flows, together, we will sway,
  Love, our guiding light, through each passing day.

Moonlit Melodies

In the soft moonlight, our love so true
  Brush my lips with a gentle, soothing melody.
  Let your touch on my skin, a melody played.

Play my body like a piano, each note a sigh.
  As we lose ourselves in this love, oh-so-high.
  Let us make love and dance the night away.

In each other's arms, forever to stay.
  Passion and grace paint our love scene.
  As we twirl and swirl in this intimate embrace
  In the rhythm of our hearts, our love will soar.
  As we dance the night away, always.

Ecstasy in moonlit haze

I could be,
   Your porn site,
   A sultry screen of ecstasy,
   Where fantasies ignite.

And, your taste of warm wine,
   Savoring the divine beverage,
   Intoxicated by the allure of your touch,
   At this moment, nothing else matters much.

It is not so dark of night,
   Or a stormy night,
   But tonight, the warm wind blows the stars around four miles.

With a friendly smile.
   Underneath the celestial display,
   Our love dances in the moonlit haze.

I am drunk,
   I am in my feelings,
   Lost in the depths of your embrace,
   Where passion has no ceilings.

It feels as if my body is a warm light,

And I tighten my feelings.
Bound by the spell of our desires,
Igniting flames that never tire.

I walk right,
   It is a long night for height,
   Underneath the velvet sky,
   Our love reaches new heights, soaring high.

Smoking Ganja boosts my sexual
   desire, ready to perform all night,
   Not four nights. In this symphony of love and lust,
   We find ourselves in each other,
   entrusting ourselves to each other.

Chapter Four

Parenthood

Opens with quotes that set the stage for a series of poems focused on the theme of parents. Each poem explores various aspects of parental relationships and experiences.

Cherishing Parenthood: From ordinary to extraordinary love

"Parenthood: where the ordinary becomes extraordinary, and the mundane becomes priceless."

"Parenthood is beautiful because of love. It is a boundless affection that grows with each moment and challenge."

Quote 1: This quote shows how the daily parts of parenthood become moments of great meaning. They become moments of worth.

Quote 2: This quote emphasizes the deep beauty of parenthood. The love parents feel is limitless. It grows with each moment and each conquered obstacle.

Band-aid-babies

It is sad,
  Like a relentless ailment with no cure.
  No perfect time to embrace a baby,
  You can start a family as a Band-Aid.

But a baby will not mend,
  A shattered bond on which we depend.
  Life's not a tale of fairy dust,
  Parenthood is more than hearts to trust.

A whirlwind of feelings, spinning 'round,
  Navigating co-parenting sound.
  Responsibility rests on your shoulders,
  Life's ember smolders.

Do not wait for others to align,
  Forge ahead, do not glance behind.
  Push toward a brighter tomorrow,
  For your child, a loving sorrows-morrow.

Shun the storm and strife,
  Focus on painting a tranquil life.

No harsh words, no malice in speech,

Love and care are within reach.

Echoes of innocence: Navigating Love's Complexities

I cherish kids, their laughter pure and bright,
    Yet, as a woman, I must tread with slight,
    For when a man with offspring comes my way,
    I regret this is not the route to pursue.

But sweet, charming, or sincere,
    If there is a child involved,
    I must veer,
    For with the father, the mother appears,
    Her drama echoes through the passing years.

It is not the child but her presence, too,
    Bringing turmoil that I cannot subdue,
    With bonds unbreakable, tangled, and deep,
    I dare not enter these waters to keep.

So, I bid farewell to this intricate dance,
    Avoiding the chaos, the fraught circumstances,
    For without common ground, peace cannot thrive,
    In this delicate balance, I strive to survive.

Seeds of tomorrow

In the journey towards tomorrow,
  Though it seems distant,
  It sneaks up,
  We observe our children's growth with intense interest.
  For they are the architects of what is to come.

We shape them,
  We nurture them,
  Instilling values deep and robust,
  Hoping these seeds will carry forward,
  The essence of our beliefs.

They are the pioneers,
  The visionaries,
  The architects of change,
  Who will shape tomorrow's landscape,
  As they blossom and grow,
  We entrust in their ability to sow.

So, let us embrace each fleeting moment,
  Let us guide with gentle hands,
  For tomorrow's promise,
  Rests in their grasp,

With boundless potential,
They will forge a world that lasts.

Guided by your love

I am grateful that you are my mother,
   Your love and warmth are a guiding light.
   Through every storm and all life's struggles,
   You are my rock, my comfort, my might.

I am thankful that you are my father,
   Your strength and wisdom are a steady hand.
   Navigating life's uncertain waters,
   You are my anchor, my shelter, my land.

My boat, a shining star in darkest times,
   Guided by your love, I navigate the waves.
   In depths of despair, your light always shines,
   The love you both gave has blessed me.

Guiding light

In the depths of my mind,
   a memory rests, obscure,
   A day I did not grasp how my life would mature.
   Yet I recall the gentle touch,
   the hands that shaped me fine,
   "Forming me like a tree, its branches intertwine."

You taught me of love and pain,
   Of trials and triumphs, joy, and disdain.
   Your wisdom led me through life's uncertain tide,
   And though my memories are few,
   Your presence was my guide.

Though I may not recall my first awakening cry,
   I know you were there as the world passed by.
   As I grew and learned to walk and stand,
   You were always present, a steadfast hand.

Thank you for all you have given me,
   For molding me into someone genuine
   and accessible. Your love and care, a beacon in the night,
   A guiding light that shines forever bright.

The wind beneath my wings

Like a bird that soars on a perfect day,
In the breeze that brings a smile my way,
You, my mom, are the gentle air,
Guiding me with loving care.

Your presence, like a bird's strong wings,
Carries me through life's stings,
With grace and tender touch,
You lift me so much.

Through stormy skies and darker times,
Your love shines, ever sublime,
Like the bird that climbs the sky,
You give me constant direction to establish lofty targets.

So, here is to you, my cherished guide,
My steadfast light, my constant pride,
In your love, I find my course,
You are the wind beneath my wings, of course.

Anchored in love: A tribute to my parents

Without my parents, where would I be?
    Adrift in a sea of uncertainty.
    They are the pillars that hold me fast.
    Their love overflowing, a boundless sea that will forever last.

My mom, my rock, a gentle guiding light.
    Her wisdom illuminates the darkest of nights.
    My dad, my hero, is strong and truthful.
    His support is a steady anchor, always holding me through.

Together, they are the miracles that are in my life.
    The reason is that I can face any struggle.
    Like the sunrise over the ocean's tide.
    Their love radiates, enveloping me in warmth and filling me with pride.

I am forever grateful for their love, so pure.
    A gift from above, endure the treasure.
    I am protected from getting lost at sea by my parents.
    But with them by my side, I am free to be.

Navigating the river of emotions: A tribute to parental love

In the river of my emotions, a gentle flow
   Moving through the sands of time,
   a peaceful show Crashing against the shores of my soul
   Yet, finding solace in the love that makes me whole.

Guided by the life jackets of my parents' care.
   Their love is a beacon, a light beyond comparison.
   Navigating the currents of life's endless tide
   With their wisdom and guidance by my side

Their love is a shelter from the raging storm.
   A haven where my emotions can transform.
   Their guidance was like a compass, leading me ashore.

Through the ebb and flow of life, always
   In their love, I find peace and solace.
   In their care, I find strength and grace.
   Anchored to their love, no matter what happens.
   I will navigate the river of emotions day by day.

Echoes of parental melody

My parent's words are like a melody,
   Echo in my mind so heavenly,
   In pure love, they are sung to me,
   Divine lyrics that set me free.

Guiding me through life's rough seas,
   Their songs of wisdom bring me peace,
   A rhythm so sweet, a melody,
   Etched in my being, a lasting mark.

Their love resounds in every line,
   Like a symphony so sublime,
   Forever cherished, always nearby,
   My parents' songs, forever dear.

Chapter Five

Self-love

Opens with a quote about self-love that sets the tone for the following poetry. The poems in this chapter explore self-acceptance. They also explore personal growth and the importance of valuing oneself. Each piece reflects distinct parts of self-love. They cover overcoming insecurities and celebrating one's worth. They create a story about the journey to self-compassion and empowerment.

Awakening potential: Embracing Self-Love and Overcoming Limits

"Embrace the beauty of self-love; it's the awakening moment that transforms life."

"Your only limit is the one you set for yourself. Push beyond it, and you'll find your true potential."

Explore the power of self-love in "Embrace the beauty of self-love." It is the awakening that transforms life. Also, explore the journey to finding your true potential in "Your only limit is the one you set for yourself." Push beyond it, and you'll find your true potential." This title captures self-love. It is about breaking limits to reach your potential.

Unseen Beacon

In a world of faceless names,
   I stand tall, my love aflame.
   Though unseen, I am not nameless.
   In my heart, my passion remains.

Through the depths of dark and light,
   I shine bright, a beacon in the night.
   My love for self, a guiding flame,
   In a world where faces may seem tame.

So, do not underestimate.
   The strength of love bears no weight.
   For though I may be unknown to you,
   My love for myself will always be true.

Celestial Fire

I may seem delicate, like a leaf.
    Adrift on the wind's gentle breath,
    Yet beneath this veneer, a fire ignites,
    A love that dazzles with celestial light.

In the quiet depths,
    I find my grace, A sense of belonging,
    wild and free.

I am not alone nor adrift in a storm.
    I am a piece of starlight where I belong.

In this grand cosmos, a mere fragment I am,
    A speck of stardust, a crafted gem.
    Though I may seem fractured,
    I am whole, A masterpiece of love, a beating soul.

In your heart, A light shines

In the quiet dawn, where dreams ignite,
The spark within is burning bright.
Though shadows loom and doubts arise,
Your spirit soars beyond the skies.

Every step makes a path.
Through trials, fierce and fears betrayed.
The mountains are high, the valleys deep,
Are but the grounds where strength will sleep.

In every fall, in every scar,
A tale of courage, near and far.
Rise with the sun, embrace the fight,
For in your heart, there shines a light.

Let failures teach, let struggles mold,
Your inner fire is pure gold.
The journey's hard, the end unclear,
But trust yourself and persevere.

For in your soul, a force untamed,
A destiny that is yet unnamed.
Embrace each moment, face the storm,
Carve out a unique direction that belongs to you alone.

True wealth

Money may rule the world's vast expanse,
   Yet not within my heart's proper state.
   For my soul harbors treasures deep,
   Whose radiance intensifies every year.

I find my worth in each passing day.
   Uncovering riches deep within.
   In cherished memories, pure affection,
   In love, which enfolds me forevermore.

Money ebbs and flows with time's sway,
   Yet my soul's richness endures,
   An immeasurable wealth remains unshaken.
   In the joy that it brings.

Let them proclaim money's reign supreme.
   Yet I know where true plenty lies,
   In the depths of my being, In love's
   boundless and timeless ties.

Resilient Health

My soul, the root of my heart,
  Torn apart and remade through dark trials,
  A ceaseless struggle, a fierce, unyielding force,
  Yet, I cherish my resilience.

In despair, I discover strength,
  My soul, weathered and scarred, stands firm,
  Guiding me through the blackest of nights,
  And I am grateful for its steadfast light.

Grounded in self-love

If my heart takes flight today,
 I will soar with the wind.
 And dance among the clouds,
 Yet, my love for myself will stay grounded.

When my spirit ventures forth,
 I will welcome the unknown
 And the journey into the beyond,
 But self-cherishing will be my guiding light.

Garden of self-acceptance

In the garden of self-love,
    I will plant. seeds of kindness and tend them with care,
    nourished by tears shed in moments of doubt,
    blossoming into a forest of self-acceptance.

Obstacles may line my path as stones,
    but I will forge a bridge with resilience and strength,
    each step is a testament to my unwavering spirit,
    a journey towards personal growth and inner peace.

Beacon Of Resilience

In the depths of despair's dark embrace,
　　I seek refuge in the light's warm grace.
　　A beacon pierces the veil of night,
　　Guiding me towards the dawn's first light.

Tears of anguish swept away,
　　As my soul, like a Phoenix, finds its way—
　　Rising from the ashes of yesterday,
　　Embracing hope's gentle, steadfast sway.

Though judgment day may not draw near,
　　Life's sweetness fills my senses.
　　Each meal a joy, each drink a cheer,
　　At this moment, I find my purpose here.

My love for self-fuels my climb,
　　To overcome each challenge, each climb.
　　I am human, resilient, and bold— No chain can bind me, no shackle hold.

Suicidal thoughts cast far aside,
　　For I am a star with a guiding light.
　　My heart beats strong, a beacon bright,
　　Leading me through the darkest night.

In the summer breeze, I find my peace,
With every breath, my worries cease.
Unstoppable, unbreakable,
I soar, A beacon of hope always.

Secrets In The Mountain Veil

In a mountain town where secrets lay,
Whispers of a love story drifted away.
Isabella, gentle, with a heart so true,
She found herself drawn to a new stranger.

A man with eyes of a sad blue,
His past was cloaked in shadows that few knew.
Yet Isabella felt a bond so deep,
As if their souls had promised to keep.

The townsfolk murmured of his dark past,
But Isabella's love was steadfast.
She yearned to unearth the truth concealed,
Believing their love could never be repealed.

As she delved into secrets entwined,
The truth emerged, leaving her mind confined.
Isabella faced a choice so stark,
To follow her heart or leave a mark.

In the mountain town where love and lore entwine,
Their tale persists in the secrets they define.
Isabella's story of a bond so profound,
Where love and mystery eternally resound.

www.ingramcontent.com/pod-product-compliance
Lightning Source LLC
Chambersburg PA
CBHW052019150726
47999CB00004B/1728